"Since 199
Carlisle utili
If you own land and are thinking of its future development, use this book as a valuable resource filled with real examples from a seasoned professional whose integrity, I might add, is second to none."
–**Paul Oddo, Founder of Oddo Brothers CPAs**

"Bruce Carlisle knows more about land than anyone I've ever met. If you own land or WANT to own land, you will find the ideas in this book extremely valuable."
–**Doug Molyneaux, Owner of the Molyneaux Group**

"I have known and worked with Bruce for many years. He understands the complexity of land transactions and works tirelessly for the owners he represents."
–**Barry Phillip "Phill" Bettis, Founding Partner of Bettis Law Group**

"As a top performer in the commercial real estate industry, the experience Bruce has amassed over his lengthy career is invaluable. His professionalism and care for his clients are two of his greatest strengths."
–**Rod Santomassimo, President of The Massimo Group**

"I've had the pleasure of working with Bruce on multiple real estate transactions since 1991, where he has represented me as both a Seller's Agent and Buyer's Agent. Bruce is a real problem solver and works diligently and creatively for his clients. Trustworthy, honest, and a one-of-a-kind land broker."
–Charlie Heard, Executive Vice President at Retail Planning Corporation

"Bruce's optimism and perseverance have led him through a lengthy career of successfully brokering many intricate transactions. I always enjoy working with him."
–Garen Smith, Vice President of Land Acquisition for a national homebuilder

"Real estate is a relational business, and the long-term success of those in our industry is marked by their character. Since 1999, I've had the pleasure to work with Bruce on various land deals. His integrity, dedication, and spirit to do the right thing for all parties is what sets him apart."
–Doug Strall, Vice President at KM Homes

"I've known Bruce since 1985, and his desire to serve and guide owners makes him a standout in the industry."
–William H. "Skip" Harper, President of Harper Southeastern Properties, Inc.

"I have worked with Bruce in the assemblage of several complicated transactions. He consistently rises to the occasion to help me creatively overcome each new obstacle."
–Woody Snell, President of Lynwood Development

"I first met Bruce in the 1980s when he sold my mother-in-law's property around Northlake Mall. In 2019, we decided to sell our family farm in Tucker, and Bruce was the only person I needed to call. Throughout the process, Bruce always put my needs above making the deal. He truly cares about his clients."
–Mary Bolton, Property Owner

"Having known Bruce since he was in high school, he has always been one to outhustle his opponents on and off the tennis court. When I hired him in 1984, I quickly realized that his high integrity, easy-going personality, competitiveness and vast knowledge would serve him well throughout his career. If you have land to sell, you should call Bruce!"
–Fred Freyer, Co-founder of Property Systems Corporation

TOP DOLLAR DIRT

13 Proven Strategies to Be a Wise Landowner

TOP DOLLAR DIRT

13 Proven Strategies to Be a Wise Landowner

Bruce M. Carlisle, CCIM

To my incredible wife Marybel and my children Zachary and Marina, thank you for the joy, encouragement, and support you have provided me throughout my life and career.

TABLE OF CONTENTS

Introduction 1

Getting Started 9

Strategy #1: The NGL Land Value Cycle 13

Strategy #2: Know And Walk Your Property 19

Strategy #3: Understand The Potential Value Sewer
Access Can Provide 33

Strategy #4: Maximize Your Ingress And Egress 39

Strategy #5: Study The Impact Of Water On Your Land....47

Strategy #6: Determine Your Property's Highest and
Best Use.. 55

Strategy #7: Density Equals Value...................................... 69

Strategy #8: Understand Local Politics 73

Strategy #9: Determine The Market Value Of Your
Property 85

Strategy #10: Evaluate Potential Tax Consequences 99

Strategy #11: Identify And Mitigate Potential Legal
Issues And Risks.. 107

Strategy #12: Negotiating Nuggets 115

Strategy #13: Select The Right Broker.............................. 121

Conclusion 131

About The Author 135

About North Georgia Land............................... 141

INTRODUCTION

THE SEASONS AND CYCLES
OF LIFE AND LAND

In the spring of 1984, at the youthful age of twenty-three, I began my commercial real estate career. I had just graduated from Florida State University and was newly engaged to my high school sweetheart. We were planning a fall wedding in September of that year, and I remember being extremely driven to succeed and provide for my new family.

Fortunately, I was quickly hired by one of the leading land brokerage companies in Atlanta—Property Systems Corporation (PSC). Property Systems, a pioneer in using critical data and analyzing trends in the land business, was founded by Fred Freyer and Richard Uberto. These two men understood the qualities and values needed to be a successful commercial land broker, and they graciously poured their knowledge and wisdom into my eager young mind.

In addition to being great with people, Fred and Richard were ahead of their time when it came to using information and data in commercial real estate. They were leaders in employing the latest software to track and analyze pertinent data to assist landowners through the process of maximizing the value of their land.

Several of the principles I will share with you in this book are rooted in the land fundamentals I was taught at PSC. I will always be indebted to Fred and Richard for the opportunity and guidance they provided me so many years ago.

Similarities Between Land and Life

As I have reflected on my life and career throughout the years, I have realized that land and life have many similarities.

To begin with, both require a long-term perspective. Just as the decisions we make early in our lives have long-term consequences, the decisions you make about your land can also dramatically impact its future value and your legacy. In both instances, it is essential to take a long-term view.

Two critical questions to ask yourself, regardless of where you are in life, are *"How do you want to be remembered?"* and *"How will the decisions you make today impact you, your family, and your land in the future?"*

Both life and land require vision and patience.

There are many reasons people buy land, bequeath it, donate it, develop it, farm it, or just enjoy it. They often have a vision for the property and the potential benefits it can bring for their family–both in creating memories and financial security.

One of my earliest memories of real estate was the sale of Spruill Farm located at I-285 and Ashford Dunwoody Road, owned by Carey Spruill. Spruill was no longer farming the land, so he initially intended to sell 90 acres to developers. After further consideration, he eventually ended up keeping 20 acres and selling the remaining 70 to developer and builder Jim Cowart.

Cowart later sold the acquisition to developer Michael Gearon, who turned around and resold it to a trio that included the Rouse Company, Richard Rich of Rich's Department Stores, and the J. C. Penney Company. The group opened Perimeter Mall in August of 1971, with Rich's and J.C. Penney as anchors on opposite ends of the mall. Rich's was ultimately acquired by Macy's in

2005. Spurred by the mall, growth quickly moved north up Georgia 400.

Retail destinations like Perimeter Mall are centers of influence that spark peripheral growth. New office buildings, apartment complexes, restaurants, and the services needed to support them begin to develop around these employment centers, which soon develop into their own trade area. As you drive around Atlanta, try to identify the various retail and non-retail employment centers. Take a moment to study the growth, opportunities, and uses that these economic drivers have created for the surrounding landowners and businesses.

In the early 2000s, the concept of live/work/play mixed-use projects came into fashion. A great example of this transformation occurred in Alpharetta with Avalon. The project was conceived in the 2000s, but its development was stymied by the Great Recession of 2008, the effects of which were felt through 2011. As a result, ownership of the Avalon site went back to multiple lenders before it was ultimately acquired by a new group and developed.

Phase I of the project finally opened in 2014, followed by Phase II in 2017. Avalon is now one of the most successful open-air, mixed-use projects in North America. The lesson—investing in land and land development requires vision, patience, capital, and long-term planning.

When it comes to your property, some questions to ask yourself include:

- What is the vision you have for your land?
- How does this vision fit into your family's legacy?
- How can you ensure that the legacy you envision for your land remains intact?

Like life, land management goes through seasons and cycles.

I got married at twenty-three and had two children by the time I was thirty. I started my brokerage company in 1993, at age thirty-three. Together, my wife Marybel and I raised our children and helped care for my aging parents. Life has been full and wonderful but not without its unpredictable bumps and bruises.

This is similar to managing land. When you purchased or inherited your property, you may have thought things would unfold in a certain way—just as you envisioned. However, rarely does that happen in life or in owning land.

One of the most critical questions a property owner should ask themselves is, *"What are the most important strategies I can employ to achieve my land's highest and best use, maximize its value, and help me create the legacy I desire?"*

We will be answering this question throughout this book.

Like life, land is impacted by economic cycles and political changes.

Sometimes these changes create challenges, while other times, they create opportunities. For instance, there was a time when multiple counties in Georgia were shut down due to a lack of sewer capacity. Understandably, the shutdown led to a dramatic decrease in demand for land in the area. Conversely, when new sewer treatment plants are constructed, or new sewer lines are installed, demand and property prices can quickly increase.

As a landowner, it is essential to understand how external forces, third parties, and regulations can affect the demand and value of your property.

In writing *Top Dollar Dirt: 13 Proven Strategies to be a Wise Landowner*, my purpose is to help you become aware of what directly impacts the value of your land and how you can proactively manage these forces.

Remember, every property is unique. The strategies I present in each chapter are conceptual but based on my experience and expertise. I recommend that you study each strategy against the context of your situation and find the ones that are the most applicable to you. As you learn more, your confidence in applying the relevant strategies will increase so you can better manage and maximize the value of your property.

In my life and in my career, my philosophy is simple, "The best is yet to come."

Keep the faith,

Bruce M. Carlisle, CCIM

GETTING STARTED

After working with landowners since 1984, I know the vast majority want to be wise stewards of their family's property. However, selling property can be complicated, and the possibility of making a mistake can make many landowners feel overwhelmed and paralyzed. The process is complex, confusing, and laden with potential pitfalls which can put one of your family's most prized assets at risk. Therefore, I decided to write this book—to help landowners gain a better understanding of the factors that impact the value of their property and learn from past property owners who have successfully managed the process.

When we begin to work with a landowner, my team and I first seek to understand the goals and objectives they have for their property. After many decades of guiding landowners through their long-term planning, we have a few high-level observations we would like to share.

- Most owners underestimate the complexity of managing and selling their land.
- If your property is owned by multiple family members, an operating agreement may be helpful for providing a structure to delineate responsibility.
- Fear and uncertainty often keep owners from making decisions. When faced with an important choice, research your options and gather as much information as possible. Consider how your options align with your goals and how they affect the various stakeholders. Once you make a decision, do not second guess yourself.
- Think about your time horizons. Unfortunately, many owners wait too long, and their health may begin to fail before they can realize their dreams and enjoy the financial benefits of selling their property. These benefits may include family vacations, supporting children and grandchildren's educational opportunities, unexpected medical expenses, long-term care, charitable donations, or just spoiling yourself.
- Many owners underestimate the problems associated with subdividing property between heirs. It is much easier to divide dollars than acres.
- Some owners expect the sales transaction timeline to move quickly. Unfortunately, the process can be tedious and takes longer than most

people realize. Rushing into a deal can cost you money.

As we have mentioned, timing is key, and successful land management requires long-term vision. Unfortunately, market timing does not always line up with a property owner's timing.

We cannot control the unforeseen life events or circumstances that affect a decision to sell.

Whether it is the death of a family member, health issues, paying for college tuition, or just a desire to turn a non-revenue-producing asset into cash, owners' motivations vary widely. Applying the strategies described in this book will help you understand the challenges and opportunities associated with managing and selling your property.

Unfortunately, I have witnessed many family feuds because owners did not seek proper legal advice and get good financial counsel. Be proactive to minimize the potential negative consequences land and the dollars it creates may have on family relationships. Manage your property wisely and build the legacy you desire.

Throughout this book, we will share numerous examples highlighting the challenges many landowners have faced and the solutions we have implemented when representing them. The specific applications will be somewhat unique to your situation.

By understanding what affects the value of your property, you will be better able to manage your land, find an advisor that aligns with your vision, and move forward with greater confidence. In this book, you will learn 13 strategies that will significantly enhance your knowledge of land stewardship and help you maximize the value of your property.

STRATEGY #1

THE NGL LAND VALUE CYCLE

In his book, *The Secret Life of Real Estate and Banking (2008/2009),* author Phillip J. Anderson identifies the average length of land valuation cycles. After studying the real estate market in the United States since the 1800s, Anderson discovered that, on average, land values move through four phases over an 18-year period. Although the time frames for the four phases vary per segment and cycle, the overall trends have been historically consistent.

Building on Anderson's work as well as a vast array of real estate research, my team and I developed our own proprietary real estate cycle. Over the years, we have found that landowners are interested in the markers that signal potential shifts in land values and demand.

Our model—*The NGL Land Value Cycle*—specifically focuses on the correlation between land values and the housing market. The four phases in our model are:

- Recovery
- Expansion
- Oversupply
- Recession

Then the cycle repeats itself.

Like the stock market, no one can predict precisely where we are in the cycle at a specific point in time. That is why we must look at trends and current market conditions to make our best assessment.

The Recovery Phase

In the Recovery Phase of the cycle, demand for land and housing is just starting to increase. Land prices are stable but are beginning to rise. Early in the phase is a good time for buyers to acquire property. As demand increases, capital becomes more available. Construction begins to escalate as well. New subdivisions are starting to be developed, and builders are optimistic that demand will continue.

The Expansion Phase

In the Expansion Phase, more developers and builders enter the market as capital is more readily available and confidence in the market grows. Land prices continue to rise, and the number of home buyers entering the market increases as well. As demand for housing exceeds the available supply, housing inventory attempts to meet the growing demand. At the peak of the cycle, land, lot, and home prices surge as a wave of consumers flood the market. Often characterized as a seller's market, this is the best time to sell your property and the worst time to buy.

The Oversupply Phase

In the Oversupply Phase, demand for new housing weakens, and the monthly supply of housing inventory available for sale begins to increase. This increase in available inventory lessens the demand and begins to lower the price for land.

The Recession Phase

In the Recession Phase, land prices decrease as builders and developers become more hesitant to take on new projects. Fewer home buyers enter the market and those that do enter the market demand more value for their dollar. The monthly supply of housing inventory continues to rise, forcing builders to slow their construction activity and potentially lower home prices. This is the best time to buy and the worst time to sell.

The Recession Phase may or may not correlate with an economic recession, and vice versa. As we saw during the COVID-19 pandemic—no doubt a black swan event—while there was a technical economic recession in 2020, demand for housing and land skyrocketed. The increase in demand created a shortage of available housing inventory and pushed prices up.

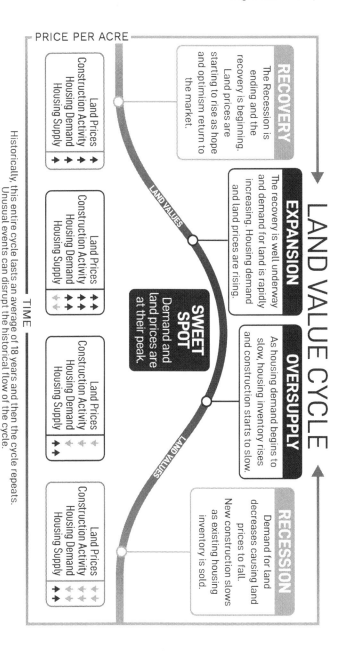

LAND VALUE CYCLE

PRICE PER ACRE

RECOVERY
The Recession is ending and the recovery is beginning. Land prices are starting to rise as hope and optimism return to the market.

Land Prices	→
Construction Activity	→
Housing Demand	→
Housing Supply	→

EXPANSION
The recovery is well underway and demand for land is rapidly increasing. Housing demand and land prices are rising.

Land Prices	→ →
Construction Activity	→ →
Housing Demand	→ →
Housing Supply	← ←

SWEET SPOT
Demand and land prices are at their peak.

OVERSUPPLY
As housing demand begins to slow, housing inventory rises and construction starts to slow.

Land Prices	→ →
Construction Activity	←
Housing Demand	←
Housing Supply	←

RECESSION
Demand for land decreases causing land prices to fall. New construction slows as existing housing inventory is sold.

Land Prices	→
Construction Activity	← ←
Housing Demand	← ←
Housing Supply	← →

LAND VALUES

TIME

Historically, this entire cycle lasts an average of 18 years and then the cycle repeats. Unusual events can disrupt the historical flow of the cycle.

STRATEGY #2

KNOW AND WALK YOUR PROPERTY

Getting to know the unique characteristics of your land is essential. Whether you have owned your property for generations or just recently acquired it, land is constantly changing along with the seasons. As time passes, your property can be impacted by rain, nearby developments, new road construction, falling trees, erosion, flooding, etc.

Some of the changes and impacts are temporary, but others are permanent. Unless you catch the changes early, they can have a detrimental effect on the land's value and marketability. It is impossible to understand how the items mentioned above may impact your land without walking your property regularly.

To that end, we recommend that you walk your property at least twice a year to review the location of the corners, determine if anything has changed, and see if any developments have the potential to become a problem. Ideal times to walk your property are after a heavy rain or after a storm. This will allow you to see how inclement weather can potentially affect your land.

For example, during or immediately after a hard rain, put on your boots and raincoat and head out to see how the water flows over your property. Ideally, I recommend that you schedule your personal surveys during the same time every year so you can see any changes more distinctly.

Additionally, winter is a great time to bundle up and walk your land. There are no spiders or snakes lurking about, the leaves are off the trees, and the undergrowth has died back, so you can see a much greater distance.

Depending on the size of your land, walking your property could be a considerable undertaking. As a result, you may have to break down the process over a few days or gather your children or other family members to help.

Some landowners may use a car, truck, or utility vehicle to get to a specific spot on their land. We encourage you to walk along property lines and view either new or existing improvements.

Some of the items that we recommend every landowner take with them include the following:

- Camera

  - o While this may seem logical, and most of us have excellent cameras on our phones, some folks may prefer to leave them behind, so we always include them on our list. A handheld camera, whether on your phone or not, will be helpful to take pictures of your property.

    Motion detection cameras can be used to identify trespassers and help determine the cause of any property damage.

    We recommend creating either digital or physical albums organized by date to capture changes that may occur on your land.

- Video

  - o Keeping a video record of your property will prove to be quite valuable. You can record how the water flows after heavy rain or how runoff may be impacting your property. As with the photos, organize your videos by date.

- Rain or mud boots

  o Whether it is raining or not, packing a pair of boots will prove useful. You may find that you want or need to wade through water or mud. If this is the case, it is best to have a designated pair of work boots you won't mind getting muddy or soaked.

- Binoculars

  o You may find binoculars quite handy in your jaunt as you peer out across your property. Some property owners enjoy the use of binoculars that offer digital recordings. Although fun, these digital recording binoculars are not a necessary tool.

- Survey and compass

  o Carry a copy of your property's survey and a compass to help keep you oriented. There are calls on your survey which will show the direction of each property line. The compass will help you get back to your starting point if you are on a large tract of land. Do not rely on your phone alone.

- Phone

  o You will want your cell phone with you for many reasons. Without any of the above tools, it will make do as a camera, video camera, flashlight, GPS, measuring tool, notes, etc. However, it may not work in all areas of your land.

    There are many reports of landowners surveying their new land or property, getting disoriented, and finding themselves without cell reception. Do not rely on your phone or memory alone to make your way back. If you are a new landowner, you may not be aware of patches on your land that do not have cell reception.

    Despite all of that, take your phone with you and make sure it is fully charged.

- Walking Stick and Pepper Spray

  o A walking stick can help you maintain your balance over rough terrain and help remove spider webs. I have a favorite walking stick I keep in my car. I also carry pepper spray just to be extra safe.

- Drones

  o Drones have added a whole new dimension to getting to know your land. Vantage points that were once only visible via heli-copter—an expensive and highly impracti-cal solution—are now easily viewed using drones. At North Georgia Land, we regu-larly utilize drones to help serve all our property owners.

EXPERIENCE FROM THE FIELD

DeKalb County Property Water Erosion

I represented a landowner whose property in DeKalb County was impacted by a new development that was being built next door.

We soon discovered that there was an exorbitant amount of water being released from the new develop-ment onto my client's property. The high volume of water started creating erosion problems that did not ex-ist prior to the new project being constructed.

My client had always been very proactive with his land and regularly walked and inspected his property. For-tunately, he had taken many pictures during heavy rains before and after the water started to be released onto his land by the new development. The photos served as evidence when my client presented his case regarding the erosion to the county and developer.

Thanks to the pictures and after several legal exchanges, the parties ultimately agreed upon a resolution that favored my client.

EXPERIENCE FROM THE FIELD

Highway 20 in Gwinnett

Several years ago, I sold a tract of land fronting Highway 20 in Gwinnett County. My client lived out of state, so when the road was widened from two lanes to four, he did not realize how the new construction would impact his property.

Typically, a road widening is welcomed in a commercially zoned area because it means more traffic and greater visibility for the property. In this case, it was especially welcomed because there was a median break in front of my client's undeveloped land allowing for full access in and out of the property. Without a median break, the property is limited to a right-in/right-out access.

While walking his property, we quickly realized there was a problem.

The road, we discovered, was designed to capture rain runoff from its surface and route it directly onto my client's land. As a result, a low-lying area on the property became classified as a *blue line creek,* and 25% of his property was deemed unusable.

Faced with this challenge, our strategy was to use the undevelopable area of the property as open space to help obtain a beneficial rezoning. The undeveloped land would be utilized as an amenity to make the project more appealing for residential development.

Fortunately for my client, our strategy was successful, and we were able to favorably rezone the property for townhomes. As a result, we also achieved a higher sales price than expected for the land.

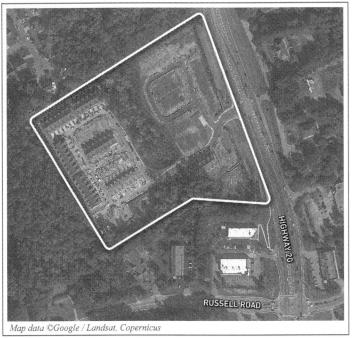

Map data ©Google / Landsat, Copernicus

Partially built-out townhome development off of Highway 20

Site plan for townhome development off of Highway 20

There are two lessons from these two experiences. From the first, we learn that whether you live in the state or out of state, it is essential to consult professionals regarding any adjacent construction that could impact your property.

In the second example, we see the importance of having an engineer review the construction plans prior to conveying any right-of-way when a road in front of your property is being widened.

In both instances, we learn that walking your property can help you find potential problems and stop them from becoming worse or find alternative solutions that could eventually prove beneficial.

LAND EVALUATION CHECKLIST

We recommend that every landowner walk their property regularly—at least twice a year. As you walk your land, take this checklist with you, and look for the following:

- Are there any rock outcroppings that will impact development costs?
- Are there any encroachments on your land? Encroachments can take the form of pedestrian or vehicular access drives, fences, or other structures.

- Has there been any dumping on your land?
- Is there evidence of trespassers on your land?
- Do you have "No Trespassing" signs posted?
- Do you have other relevant warning signs in cases of high voltage, surveillance, security, and danger? To protect yourself, post the signs even though you think no one will trespass.
- Are there any utility easements on your property?
- Do you have copies of your survey, easements, and other legal documents easily accessible but safely stored with backup copies?
- Is your property being reasonably well-maintained? The general appearance of your land can impact its desirability.
- Are there areas experiencing excessive erosion?
- Are there dead or dying trees that may fall on your neighbor's land? Or are there any dead or dying trees on your land? If so, could they pose a threat?
- Have drainage ditches been created?
- What path does running rain or other water form, and does it need to be redirected to minimize the impact? Could a little grading help with the drainage?
- Are there things that could be considered an attractive nuisance and attract kids or teens and

potentially cause harm? (See Strategy 11 for more details on attractive nuisances.)

Considerations

1. Nearby developments

If you are aware of any upcoming new developments on adjacent land, it may be a good idea to consult an engineer or land planner. When you walk your land, consider the impact of these new developments. Remember, the consequences may not be immediately apparent, so you will want to understand the potential repercussions. Be aware of the size of buffers and setbacks relative to new developments. These are established at the time of rezoning and should be discussed during that process.

2. Better safe than sorry

Make sure to walk your property with a family member or friend. Design the route you intend to walk before heading out. Have significant landmarks in mind, such as creek crossings or spring heads, to help you stay oriented.

Be prepared with the necessary tools described in Strategy #2 to document your findings and capture pictures along the way. Let someone know where you are going and when to expect your return. This may seem overly cautious but taking these precautions—especially if you're venturing into an unfamiliar or large area—is a wise decision.

3. Muddled memory

While you take pictures and video, be sure to save them in dated digital or physical folders, as noted earlier. If you are conducting regular walks, you may get the dates and times of findings confused.

Save your notes and all other data from the same walk in one folder. As you saw in my earlier example, this habit could prove to be beneficial in the future if an issue arises. In addition, having your images organized by date will facilitate the process of comparing changes over time that may be taking place on your property.

Key Takeaways

1. Schedule a walking tour of your property at least two times a year.
2. Document any changes found on your land.

3. Consult a professional early if you suspect nearby developments could impact your land.

STRATEGY #3

UNDERSTAND THE POTENTIAL VALUE SEWER ACCESS CAN PROVIDE

Obtaining sewer access can add a great deal of value to your undeveloped land. To secure sanitary sewer access, start by researching your city or county's local water and sewer maps. Then, schedule an appointment with the water and sewer department serving your property. They will help you identify where the closest sewer and water lines are located and determine if sewer can be provided to your property.

Be aware that in some cases, achieving access may require obtaining one or several sewer easements. The water and sewer department will also determine the size of the sewer and water lines needed in your area.

If you are planning to develop your property or are considering selling your land, it is essential to know if the sewer treatment facility that serves your property has adequate capacity to handle new developments.

Typically, when counties install sewer lines, they understand that increased densities will follow and they consider that in relation to capacity. With more density and sewer capacity comes increased land value.

From an investment perspective, purchasing land in the path of growth that will ultimately be served by sewer with adequate capacity is a winning combination.

EXPERIENCE FROM THE FIELD

The South Fork Sewer Solution

I recently worked on a property located in DeKalb County.

Unfortunately, DeKalb had deferred the maintenance of many of their sanitary sewer lines. As a result, the lines located in the South Fork Peachtree Creek sewer basin were particularly impacted, creating a unique challenge for my client and a potential developer. Even though the sewer plant had adequate capacity to serve the property, the sewer lines did not.

The buyer we chose to work with was familiar with the sewer department in DeKalb County and was told that the sewer lines within the South Fork Peachtree Creek area were overcapacity. As a result, there was no capacity available within certain sewer lines during peak times of the day.

Our team strategized with the county to come up with a creative solution to the capacity problem and devised a plan to install holding tanks on the property. The holding tanks would allow sewage to be pumped out during non-peak hours—between one and five in the morning—when there was less demand on the sewer lines.

The tanks represented an added cost to the builder, but it was the only way the property could be developed within the South Fork Sewer Basin. In the end, we developed a creative and economically viable solution to help our client sell their land.

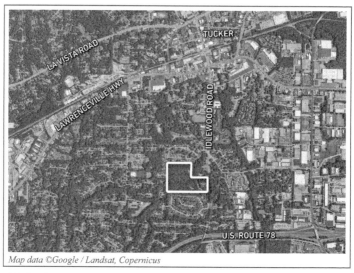

Map data ©Google / Landsat, Copernicus

WATER AND SEWER CHECKLIST

Water and sewer issues that can impact the value of your property may not be immediately evident. Here is a checklist to get you started.

Items to obtain from your local utility department:

- Location, size, and capacity of the sewer and water lines
- The route required to connect to your property
- Sewer treatment plant capacity
- Any expansion plans for the sewer plant
- Any plans for new sewer lines being installed

Key Takeaways

1. Obtaining water and sewer access adds tremendous value to your property.
2. If the sewer plant serving your property has limited capacity, you may want to consider selling sooner rather than later.
3. Determine if any new sewer lines are proposed that could serve your property.
4. Be open to creative solutions.

STRATEGY #4

MAXIMIZE YOUR INGRESS AND EGRESS

Securing optimal access to your property is an essential strategy to add value to any future development. The more access you have, the better. Keep in mind, however, that frontage does not always equal access. Just because a property fronts an interstate does not mean you have access to the interstate.

Easy and convenient access for retail development is paramount to a great retail site. If access is inconvenient, consumers will simply go elsewhere. If your land and the immediate area is undeveloped, you are at an advantage. It is always better to secure and plan access to your property prior to development. This will allow you the opportunity to work with your neighbors and fellow landowners as opposed to working with a more difficult retail developer that has a fast-food restaurant, bank, or gas station tenant.

For larger subdivisions, it is essential to have multiple access points for emergency response vehicles such as police and fire, overall safety, and convenience for residents. Explore the contiguous properties surrounding your land and determine if there is a benefit to negotiating an access easement through neighboring sites. Once again, it is better to secure any easements before a project is developed. This will allow you to better plan for and create any necessary alternative solutions for access, convenience, safety, and visibility.

A vital step to proactively managing your property's access is to meet with local planners and determine if there are any road improvements planned in the vicinity of your property. If the local government is indeed planning improvements, determine the project's timeline and research any public discussions and information relative to the project.

Remember that you can negotiate with the agency in charge to secure the best possible access for your property. If you choose to improve your site's access, be sure to get a sense of where your neighbors stand on the issue and take a big-picture approach.

There could be an opportunity to work together to increase your political clout or offer other benefits to the community that could sway the outcome in your favor. These community benefits could include median cuts, traffic lights, or other ingress and egress alternatives.

When negotiating with the authorities, access can sometimes be obtained by having the municipality install a curb cut to serve your land. This can be a great benefit.

Work with the county or the Department of Transportation to establish the final grade of the road as it relates to your property. This will make it easier to access your land by offering an entrance to your property without a steep incline or decline.

Lastly, as you saw in the example in Strategy #2, if a new road is being constructed or an existing road is being widened, water runoff from the road could be diverted onto your property causing damage to your land and adversely impacting value. Consult an engineer and have them evaluate the plans for any potential water runoff or other hidden pitfalls.

EXPERIENCE FROM THE FIELD

Ronald Reagan Boulevard Mixed-Use Project

Several years ago, I represented a family that owned eight acres at the corner of Ronald Reagan Boulevard and Brannon Road in Forsyth County.

The property has incredible visibility, but due to the median located on Ronald Reagan Boulevard, the property's access was limited to a right-in/right-out. From a retail standpoint, that greatly limited the property's value for higher-paying retailers like banks, gas stations, and restaurants.

To solve the problem, our strategy was to join forces with the owners of the contiguous tracts of land and formulate a plan that would benefit everyone. Our proposal to the county was to develop several of the adjacent properties into a major mixed-use project.

The project would create destination shopping for the area with upgraded and cohesive signage, amenities such as benches and walking paths, and unified construction materials. In addition, the new project would offer increased walkability adding tremendous value to the community and creating a market premium for the property.

The county liked the approach and supported the mixed-use rezoning for the new development. The access via a median break on Ronald Reagan Boulevard served everyone's interest.

This solution was a win/win for my client (the seller), the developer, and the community at large.

Map data ©Google / Landsat, Copernicus

Aerial image of property assemblage on Ronald Reagan Boulevard designed to include medical office space, retail, single-family detached homes, and townhomes

PROPERTY ACCESS CHECKLIST

Securing the best possible access to your property is a key ingredient to adding value. It is most critical for retail development. Here is a checklist of questions to ask yourself when evaluating access to your property.

- If your property is on a major thoroughfare, is it accessible via a main intersection with a traffic light?
- If a road in front of your property is going to be widened, will that road ultimately be above the grade of your property or below it? This is important to ensure good visibility and easy ingress and egress.
- If they plan to widen the road, will they install a median down the center of the road that could potentially prohibit left turns into your property? Will any water runoff be diverted onto your property?
- Can you work together with neighboring landowners to find an access solution that benefits everyone?
- What could help you make the case for access? Can you exchange a sewer easement for an access easement or vice versa?

Considerations

1. Road improvements

Be proactive related to any road improvements that are planned near your property. This could create an opportunity for you to secure easier and more convenient ingress and egress to your land. Do your homework, check with the proper authorities, and present your case.

2. Impact

All development projects have an impact. If the road is being widened or otherwise improved, or a new development is being considered next to your property, think about how this could impact your land. Aside from the water runoff discussed in Strategy #2, other considerations include rezoning, access, convenience, safety, and visibility.

3. Long-term Perspective

You may recall that in my introduction I stated that land ownership and stewardship can sometimes be like life and that both require a long-term perspective. As you consider access to your property, look at the big picture. For example, if a new project adjacent to your land is about to get started, does it make sense to be a part of the development? After completion, it might be too late to make any changes on elements that could impact the value of your property.

Key Takeaways

1. Meet with your local transportation department.
2. Secure access as early as possible.
3. Look at the big picture and maintain a long-term perspective.

STRATEGY #5

STUDY THE IMPACT OF WATER ON YOUR LAND

Lakes, ponds, creeks, streams, and floodplains on your property can negatively affect the acreage available for development.

Every jurisdiction establishes setbacks and buffers measured from these water features, which affect the amount of property that can be developed and how it can be utilized. These setbacks and buffers can, depending on the municipality, range from 50-75 feet from either the top of the bank or the centerline of the creek. This can equate to an approximately 150-foot-wide swath of land that cannot be developed—a significant amount of property if a stream or creek meanders through your land.

Depending on where your property is located and the controlling municipality's ordinances, this land may or may not be used to calculate density. To avoid any surprises, it is essential to understand your municipality's rules relative to calculating density on land with streams, lakes, or floodplains.

Water on your land brings with it other issues that could be of concern, such as flooding during rainy seasons, high water tables, contaminated groundwater, unwanted animals and pests, and creating an unsuitable environment for development on portions of your property.

According to the Georgia Department of Natural Resources' Wildlife Resource Division, beavers can be found statewide wherever suitable habitat exists. Beavers can build dams that can create wetlands where there were not any previously. Their dams can also flood bottomlands, pastures, or crops. This can cause significant damage to your property, so be sure to control the beaver population on your land.

As recommended in Strategy #2, walking your property after heavy rain will allow you to see if there is flooding or runoff from adjacent properties. You can also see if there is evidence of contamination, erosion, or invasive animals on your land.

Also, keep in mind that water elements can be found above and below ground. Not all water elements will be visible, and a typical land survey does not reveal a high water table.

EXPERIENCE FROM THE FIELD

Cherokee County Creativity

Several years ago, I sold a property in Cherokee County.

We had the property under contract to a national homebuilder who, during their due diligence period, discovered a high water table on a portion of the property that created unsuitable soils. The soils could not support traditional housing foundations. The builder proposed hauling away the poor soils and then importing new soils to fill the area. The entire process would have cost $975,000.

The homebuilder wanted the property owner to reduce their price by the entire $975,000. Because of the proposed reduced sales price, we terminated the agreement with the homebuilder and contracted with a new buyer.

The second buyer confirmed that the poor soils were an issue. His solution, however, was to install several French drains to lower the high water table and dry out the bad soils. Once the bad soils were dried out and the water table was lowered, the soils were removed and used to create landscape berms. No soils were required to be imported or exported. This solution cost $85,000, allowing my client to keep the $890,000 difference.

Every property will have a unique set of challenges. This case illustrates that there are multiple ways to solve challenges related to water and land development. Creativity is essential.

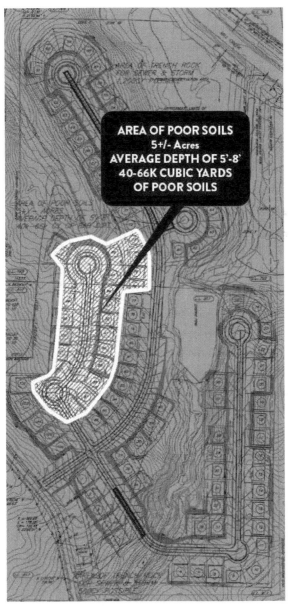

5+/- acres of poor soils

Cute but not your friend
Photo Credit: Pixaby

WATER IMPACT CHECKLIST

Regular inspections of your property are essential to control your property's potential for water or water-related damage. Here is a checklist to take with you on your inspection.

1. What water elements do you have on your property?
2. Do you see evidence of contamination or pollution? Are there any unusual colors in the water?
3. Is the area attracting beavers?
4. Is there evidence of erosion or destabilization that could be caused by water patterns on your property?

5. Are you experiencing runoff from neighboring properties?
6. Does your property flood in heavy rains?
7. What are your city or county's regulations regarding water feature setbacks and/or buffers? Will these regulations impact your property's density?

Considerations

1. **Creativity is essential.**

   Do not assume that there is only one solution to water-related issues. There are often a variety of ways to solve the same problem.

2. **Water can be found above or below ground.**

   Not all water is visible, and water below the surface can have repercussions on the value of your land or on potential development.

3. **Water can eat away at your land.**
   Erosion, setbacks, buffers, floodplains, and wetlands can affect the value of your land. Make note of these factors so that you can take appropriate action.

Key Takeaways

1. Walk your property after heavy rain.
2. Get creative when it comes to finding solutions.
3. If you have a lake or pond on your property, consult professionals about your options.

STRATEGY #6

DETERMINE YOUR PROPERTY'S HIGHEST AND BEST USE

The Appraisal Institute defines the highest and best use of real estate as follows: *the reasonable, probable, and legal use of vacant land or an improved property, which is physically possible, appropriately supported, financially feasible, and that results in the highest value.*

To determine your property's highest and best use, study the surrounding developments and activities. Start by researching the zonings and existing/future land use plans that the city or county may have for your submarket. In addition, study the rezoning cases contiguous to your property and within the immediate area. These could indicate possible avenues and opportunities for your property.

When considering your property's highest and best use, I recommend thinking outside the box. Get creative and look for what is the greatest potential need in the immediate area. If you are planning on selling your land, brainstorm who could benefit the most and gain the greatest value from your property. These potential buyers are the ones that will be willing to pay the most for your land.

Employment centers, centers of influence, and amenities such as new schools, hospitals, large corporate headquarters, a new stadium, or major distribution centers can significantly increase demand for restaurants, office space, apartments, townhomes, and single-family projects.

In addition, as a town grows, so does the need for more green spaces, connectivity, access, parks, schools, and community spaces. Your property's location could be the ideal site to connect a multi-family development or subdivision with a large retail or entertainment center.

As you seek to determine your property's highest and best use, consider your city or county's potential interests and needs. These could reveal pathways to creative uses. For example, hospitals, schools, and parks are uses that are sometimes overlooked.

Research all zoning overlay districts, special zoning designations, or nodes of activity that could impact how you can develop your property. Some municipalities designate corridors or intersections with overlay districts or activity nodes to control the uses and the architectural aesthetics associated with the region.

To gain insight into what projects are being planned and what the needs of your city, county, and community are, get involved and attend city, county, and/or community planning and zoning meetings. In addition, visit your local chamber of commerce to gain added insight into your local community.

You can also research your city or county's future land use plan to determine the long-term vision for your specific region. We will discuss local politics more in depth in Strategy #8.

EXPERIENCE FROM THE FIELD

City of Suwanee Town Center: A Family's Lasting Legacy

Several years ago, the City of Suwanee in Gwinnett County began developing a retail and entertainment destination in their downtown area, the Suwanee Town

Center. There is an amphitheater, restaurants, several retailers, and multiple housing options connected with walkable paths.

Located on prime real estate just to the southwest of the town center was the Suwanee Lumber Company, the oldest company in the city. The developing town center created a unique opportunity for the family that owned the lumber company to help leave a legacy for the town, which they deeply cared about. I had the privilege of guiding the family through the process of achieving the highest and best use for their property. This led to them obtaining the maximum price for their land.

We determined that the highest and best use for the land was a mixed-use project that included townhomes, retail, apartments, and a parking deck enhanced by open spaces and a system of walking trails.

We laid out a comprehensive strategy that involved annexing and rezoning the lumber yard so that we could sell it to a mixed-use developer. The process was complicated due to the demands of the city, the creeks flowing through the property, a need for additional municipal parking, the widening of Buford Highway, and the desire by the local government for a certain amount of open space.

We successfully navigated the process and sold the property to the ideal mixed-use developer. It was a win/win for everyone involved.

Foot traffic greatly increased at Suwanee Town Center, new residences were built, more parking was available for consumers, and the town's walking trails were greatly improved. In addition, Suwanee has done an excellent job planning and hosting concerts and creating an array of events and experiences to draw people to their town. Well done, Suwanee!

"For years we had constantly been approached about selling our 18 acres in Suwanee. When Bruce reached out to us in 2015, we knew something was different about his approach. Our property had streams running through it, a big road widening project was planned along our frontage, and the City wanted to control how our property was to be developed. In addition, we needed to relocate our business and stay in the city of Suwanee. Bruce worked alongside us through the entire project. We were able to work through every issue. In 2017, we sold our property, and we have now relocated to a new and better facility. We were blessed by how it all worked out. Bruce did a great job."
–Suwanee Lumber Co.

Suwanee Lumber Yard Property in 2017

Suwanee Lumber Yard Property in 2021

EXPERIENCE FROM THE FIELD

From office buildings to townhomes

The City of Dunwoody, located just off I-285, is a thriving community with a vast array of property types, growing businesses, and expanding residential areas. In the early years, the center of Dunwoody was located at the intersection of Mount Vernon Road and Chamblee Dunwoody Road.

To the east was an eight-acre office complex consisting of four Williamsburg-style office buildings. We identified this property as a redevelopment opportunity and approached the owner.

We soon learned that the property had previously been under contract with a developer who was unable to solve the complex engineering and zoning problems associated with redevelopment. The situation was further complicated because any changes required extensive political negotiations with the Dunwoody Homeowners Association. In addition, several of the buildings had office tenants that would require a buyout of their leases. To say that it was a complex deal is putting it mildly.

We worked hard to gain the seller's confidence and brought in a well-qualified buyer. The last point to be negotiated centered around a tenant who had three years left on his lease and refused to leave.

One strategy we considered was phasing the project and waiting out the holdout tenant. Unfortunately, this was not ideal. We modified the plan and were able to successfully negotiate a buyout provision acceptable to the tenant. The deal allowed all the property to be developed in the most efficient manner and at the same time.

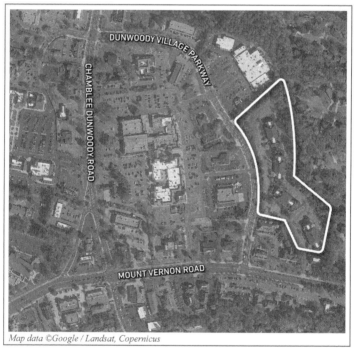

Map data ©Google / Landsat, Copernicus

Four Williamsburg-style office buildings along
Dunwoody Village Parkway

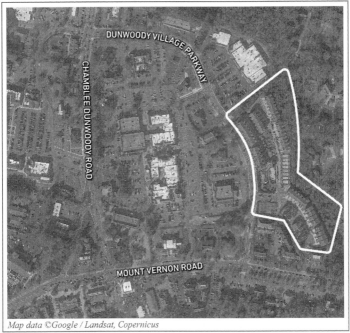

High-end townhome redevelopment along
Dunwoody Village Parkway

EXPERIENCE FROM THE FIELD

Ariana Home Furnishings

Located at the southeast corner of Georgia 400 and
Peachtree Parkway was a five-acre tract of undeveloped property. When we first looked at the property,
the highest and best use appeared obvious. It seemed to
be the perfect location for a gas station, fast food restaurant, or bank.

As we studied the access to the property more closely, however, we determined that the property was not ideally suited for an impulse purchase retailer or a convenience-driven service business. The property had terrific visibility but was difficult to access. As a result, we concluded that the highest and best use was for a destination retailer, a sit-down restaurant, or a hotel. These uses require excellent visibility, but ease of access is not essential.

We ultimately sold the property to Ariana Home Furnishings, a luxury furniture and high-end decor store featuring designer brands. Consumers do not impulsively buy luxury home furnishings. When they decide to purchase these items, local consumers think of Ariana Home Furnishings because of its excellent exposure and visibility.

This location has excellent visibility as you exit Georgia 400 onto Peachtree Parkway heading south but has limited access.

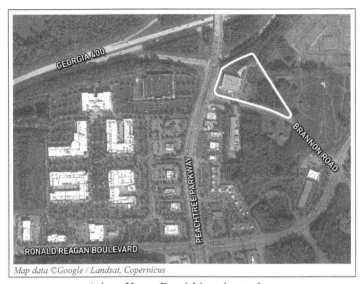

Ariana Home Furnishings located on
Peachtree Parkway and Brannon Road

Follow the black dashed line to understand the access to the
property coming off of Georgia 400.

HIGHEST AND BEST USE CHECKLIST

Identifying your property's highest and best use can significantly impact marketability, perceived value, and price. Here is a checklist of questions you can use to zero in on the potential uses and opportunities that will deliver the highest value for the prospective buyer, and as a result, the highest returns for you—the prospective seller.

- What kind of use logically fits the area?
- Who could benefit the most from acquiring your property?
- What are the most immediate needs of your community, city, or county?
- Are tax abatements or credits available?
- Are there new employment centers or centers of influence coming to your area?
- What are the area's demographic trends?
- Is the area transitioning in a positive or negative manner?
- Are incomes generally rising or falling?
- Are properties being well-maintained, or are they being neglected?
- How do the schools in the area compare to other schools?

o Tip: Check out greatschools.com to rank the schools in your area and see how they compare to other schools in your state. Schools have a significant impact on demand and value. Apartment builders look at the quality of the elementary schools, while single-family detached home builders tend to focus more on the quality of the high schools.

Considerations

1. **Probable Land Use.** Examine the surrounding area and consider the most probable and beneficial use for your property. This is a starting point to find the potential highest and best use for your land, which may ultimately include a mix of uses.

2. **Trends.** Employment, demographic, income, and development trends can impact the demand for your property. Be on the lookout for new trends that may be emerging in your community. Over the last ten years, creative greenways, beltlines, and exercise paths have proven to be influential drivers to obtaining higher land and home values.

3. **Needs.** Identifying the needs of local stakeholders, including new businesses, local governments, and your community, will take you a long way in determining your property's highest and best use.

Key Takeaways

1. Understand the most probable and beneficial use for your property.
2. Get involved with your chamber of commerce to stay well informed.
3. Think creatively. Are there any not-so-obvious uses that might be worth considering? For example: a school, park, hospital, self-storage center, parking garage, or distribution center.

STRATEGY #7

DENSITY EQUALS VALUE

Density is defined as the number of houses or units per acre that can be zoned on a property. Even if a property is zoned for many units, the physical constraints of the property may limit the actual number of units that can be built. For example, a property with a major floodplain or severe topography may be zoned for more units than can be developed on the land.

Present and future density will always determine value. With that in mind, begin to study the zoning within your submarket. You can obtain a copy of your area's future land use plan to understand the county or city's vision and growth plans.

In your area, you may conclude that your property's highest and best use is for residential development. However, it is important to note that builders and developers value land on a *per unit* basis as opposed to a *per acre* basis.

As a result, maximizing a property's density plays a critical role in valuing property for development. With that in mind, you can get a feel for potential density based upon the zoning surrounding you. If the zoning category estimates a density of 2.5 homes per acre, finding comparable sales at or near that density is ideal.

For example, land that is developed at a density of 1.5 lots per acre may be worth either $20,000 per lot or $30,000 per acre. Land that is developed at 2.5 lots per acre may be worth the same $20,000 per lot, but the value per acre is now $50,000. Larger lots do not always equate to a higher price per lot. As discussed in Strategy #5, density can be limited by streams, floodplains, steep topography, or rock formations, so be sure to check your local regulations for more information.

When given an opportunity to increase the density of your property, we strongly recommend that you take whatever action is necessary to secure that density. As areas become more populated, it becomes much more difficult to obtain higher density classifications.

EXPERIENCE FROM THE FIELD

Timing is Everything

Several years ago, a family that owned approximately 250 acres decided to sell their land.

The property had frontage on a state route and had access to all the necessary utilities. In addition, the property had an active adult community contiguous with their land at a density of six units per acre.

Unfortunately, when they chose to sell, the local political environment had dramatically shifted to an anti-growth sentiment. As a result, the density of their property was limited to between 1.5 and 2 units per acre.

Several years earlier, the property could have potentially been rezoned to a higher density classification allowing them to achieve up to 100 more lots than what was approved at the time of the sale. Had they rezoned their property earlier when the political environment was more favorable, their selling price would have been approximately $3,000,000 higher.

Key Takeaways

- Strive to maximize your property's density even before it is ready to be sold. Density equals value.

- Use the political environment to your advantage.
- Remember that builders and developers value land on a *per unit* basis as opposed to a *per acre* basis.

STRATEGY 8
UNDERSTAND LOCAL POLITICS

When it comes to land use, rezoning, and permitting, all decisions are made at the local or municipal level. Understanding how the local governing bodies work is an essential component for creating and maintaining value.

Local agencies, such as the city council or a county's board of commissioners, have the value of your land in their hands. They are responsible for land use planning, zoning, permitting, tax abatements, utility development, new roads, and many other factors that could impact the value of your property.

When considering buying or selling land it is essential to know if county commissioners or city council members are generally pro-development or anti-development. In addition, familiarize yourself with how they have voted on key development projects in the past and what new projects are in the works.

Many land investors have found it to be a particularly beneficial strategy to acquire land in the natural path of growth. This allows the investor to benefit from the momentum created by projects in the early stages of development.

To better understand how things work, who the players are, and what the development dynamics and politics are like, attend public planning and zoning meetings. Going to these meetings will offer excellent insight into the current political development trends, who is voicing concerns about specific projects and what those concerns are, and how projects or changes are presented to the public. In addition, you can meet active local business owners, public representatives and politicians, and other people of influence.

As with any topic that touches upon politics, there are public conversations and movers and shakers behind the scenes. By getting to know the people who could impact your land, you go from being a faceless landowner to becoming an involved community member.

This is an essential element in protecting your property's value.

Regularly talk with your neighbors, shop at their stores, stop by their businesses, and send them referrals. When new developments are being discussed, ask questions, request pertinent information, and share information. While you may not be a politician, this is your way of shaking hands and staying visible. Although this can be time-consuming, knowing the lay of the land and how to get things done in your local community is a critical component to maximizing your property's value.

If you live out of state, make it a point to do some hand-shaking on visits to your property. You will be amazed how far this will get you and the goodwill you will build with the other members of your community. This goodwill could mean the difference between getting a phone call or not getting a phone call to let you know that a trespasser was on your land, that a new retailer was entering the market, or alert you to anything else that could impact your property.

Keep in mind that as communities grow, conversations ebb and flow, and local leaders change. In addition, local politics, economic and social needs, new retailers, investors, developers, long-standing norms, and community demographics all shift over time and affect trends in land use.

An example of shifts that can occur is the rollout of distribution centers to support Amazon and other e-commerce growth accelerated by the COVID-19 pandemic that swept across the country.

Be sure to stay in touch, connected, and informed over the long term to maximize opportunity, information, and value.

EXPERIENCE FROM THE FIELD

Cherokee County Leadership Change

Several years ago, a small city in Cherokee County was welcoming growth and new residential projects.

The county has excellent schools, good roads, and plenty of sewer capacity. However, after several of our new projects were rezoned and developed, town residents were growing increasingly disgruntled by the traffic congestion and the rising number of students in their schools. As opposition to new developments grew, residents promptly voted the mayor out of office at election time, and the city's growth was dramatically slowed.

This example demonstrates the typical ebb and flow of development throughout the suburbs of North Atlanta. It highlights why it is critical to understand your county and city's local politics and emphasizes the importance of timing relative to rezoning. When considering selling your land, timing and politics play a pivotal role in your property's value.

Below are two properties we sold in Cherokee County.

Map data ©Google / Landsat, Copernicus

96-acre assemblage known as
Edgewater Subdivision on Hickory Road in Cherokee County

Map data ©Google / Landsat, Copernicus

The Darby apartment complex located on
Holly Springs Parkway in Cherokee County

EXPERIENCE FROM THE FIELD

The Power of a Mayor

A small community in North Georgia was controlled
by a mayor for more than three decades.

During his tenure, no decisions were made without his
approval. This dramatically limited new residential development, restricted growth, and stymied opportunity.

It was only when the city's leadership changed that new developments and growth opportunities became viable. Multiple mixed-use projects were proposed, investors entered the market, and a new city center was planned and being developed as of the printing of this book. This change prompted an increase in demand for properties and caused prices to increase.

EXPERIENCE FROM THE FIELD

The Value of Selling to the Government
Gwinnett College

In 1994, I was approached by a developer friend who asked me to broker a highly confidential land purchase.

The Board of Regents had determined that Gwinnett County was in need of a four-year college. Due to the high-profile nature of the land purchase, and the potential that the landowner could increase the price of their property, my developer friend was hired to purchase the property and assign the contract to Gwinnett County at closing.

Because the county was the ultimate purchaser, there were no concerns related to rezoning, permitting, road improvements, or obtaining utilities. Gwinnett County controlled them all.

I have sold several properties to counties for new schools. The following benefits are worth considering:

- There is no financing contingency
- There is no zoning contingency
- There is no utility contingency
- They can close relatively quickly

This example illustrates the need for you or your broker to stay involved in your local politics so you can be aware of overcrowding schools and the need for new locations.

Gwinnett County is willing to roll dice to win college

By MARK MELTZER

Special to The Post

GWINNETT CO. – Gwinnett County agreed to spend nearly $6 million on a land purchase, based on a verbal assurance that doing so very likely would bring the county its first four-year college, according to Gwinnett Commissioner Tommy Hughes.

"We were approached by some people who said that if we offer a tract of land to the Board of Regents, we'd stand a good chance of getting a four-year college," Hughes said.

The county acquired a 180-acre tract of land earlier this month for $5,948,209.

Earlier, Hughes said, he met informally with three members of the Board of Regents to discuss the idea of Gwinnett buying the land and donating it for a four-year college.

"They seemed to lead us to believe they would look favorably on it," Hughes said.

Hughes said he couldn't remember which members of the 16-member Board of Regents were at the meeting, but he said two were male and one was female.

Hughes' secretary could not supply a date for the meeting, and the county clerk said she had no record of it.

Hughes said the meeting was arranged by Virgil Williams, an influential businessman who served on the Board of Regents for six months in 1993.

Williams said he arranged a social meeting for the Gwinnett Commission "to inform the Regents of the need for a four-year college in Gwinnett," but that he knew nothing about any discussion of a land donation.

He said several simultaneous discussions were going on during the gathering.

The Gwinnett Commission announced June 22 that it had purchased an option to buy the land, and it completed the transaction July 7. Hughes said

> *'We were approached by some people who said that if we offer a tract of land to the Board of Regents, we'd stand a good chance of getting a four-year college.'*   *Gwinnett Commisioner Tommy Hughes*

the county couldn't simply retain the option to buy the land, without committing to the nearly $6 million purchase because "the landowner just wasn't going to have his land tied up."

In fact, landowner Ruth Yancey gave the county a 1 percent discount for closing the sale quickly, according to a county statement.

Georgia Gwinnett College announced in The Gwinnett Daily Post

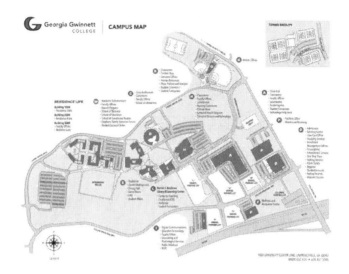

Georgia Gwinnett College Campus Map

UNDERSTANDING LOCAL POLITICS CHECK-LIST

Communities grow, conversations ebb and flow, and local leaders change. Be sure to stay connected and informed. Use this checklist as a starting point to get the lay of the local political landscape.

- Is your property governed by city or county regulations?
- Do you know in which district your property is located and who your district commissioner is?
- When do the local governing agencies hold their public meetings?
- How have they voted in the past?

- Is the county or city where your property is located generally friendly toward development? Do they want to encourage growth or discourage it?
- Is your property contiguous with the city limits, and could it potentially be annexed into the city? If so, would that be desirable?
- Who is on your area's board of commissioners, city council, and planning commission? If you do not know, visit the city or county's website. It should offer a complete list of its members.
- Who have been the loudest groups or people opposing development in the past? What are their concerns?
- What are your area's greatest social and economic needs?
- What kind of tax abatements have been issued in your county, city, or state?

Key Considerations

1. Ebb and flow

Politics and issues ebb and flow as administrations change. Therefore, take into account the current environment and relevant time horizons when considering acquiring or selling a property.

2. Out-of-state not out-of-mind

If you are an out-of-state owner, staying present and visible is especially important. Stay in touch, visit your property, and attend public meetings when possible. It is essential to develop local relationships with people in the know who can keep you abreast of critical changes. This is a great job for a local broker.

3. Influencers

Influence and politics are multi-layered and have far-reaching impact. Not all influencers are political, and not all politicians are influential or relevant to you. Understanding who the influencers are and what their views are on growth and development is essential.

Key Takeaways

1. Get involved or have a representative stay involved on your behalf.
2. Attend city, county, and/or community planning and zoning meetings.
3. Know the key players and the growth trends in your area.

STRATEGY #9

DETERMINE THE MARKET VALUE
OF YOUR PROPERTY

L andowners acquire land for a myriad of reasons. You may have inherited it, bought it with the goal of selling it, you may intend to develop it, farm it, or pass it down to your children. Regardless of why you acquired the property and where you are in the property's life cycle, having a clear understanding of what impacts the value of your land is a critical component of land stewardship.

Many factors impact the market value of your property. These factors, while fundamental, are constantly changing and can be affected by unforeseen circumstances. To stay within the scope of this book, I will focus on the factors that influence value in relation to undeveloped land or land with structures that have reached functional obsolescence.

Supply and demand for land are influenced by various factors, including the following:

- **Location, Location, Location**

  As land in desirable locations is developed, the price of undeveloped land increases. As the supply decreases and demand increases, prices rise. Hence, as you travel further from a city center, major employment center, or interstate, the price of land will decrease.

- **Desirability Trends**

  Housing and city development trends can affect your property's value. For example, tiny houses and entire rental communities of single-family homes are trends that emerged and changed the way developers and builders use land.

- **Walkability and Amenities**

  Walkability is a measure of how easy it is to walk from one place to another in a specified area. Properties can now be assigned a walka-bility score as a reflection of their easy access to desired amenities. These community amenities include greenways, amphitheaters, restaurants, shopping opportunities, and more. If your property is near some of these desired locations, the value of your property could increase. A perfect example was the Suwanee Lumber Yard Property referenced in Strategy #6.

- **Employment Centers**

  As we have reviewed in previous chapters, new businesses and employment centers, or the lack thereof, can affect the value of your property. New employment centers may increase the demand for housing and other amenities such as restaurants and support services.

  Reach out to your local government entities and chamber of commerce to better understand how the business and employment landscape is developing in your area.

  Remember that employment centers are not only office-based or professional business services. They could include a hospital, a new university campus, a distribution center, an outlet mall, and other businesses or organizations.

- **Local Politics**

  The governing body overseeing your submarket is responsible for future land use planning, zoning, permitting, tax abatements, utility development, new roads, and many other factors that could impact the value of your property. By studying their plans, you can better understand the market value of your land. For more information on navigating your local politics, see Strategy #8.

- **Utilities**

  Sewer increases value. If your property already has access to sewer, your property's value in the market will be higher than a property that does not have access. Refer to Strategy #3 for more information.

- **Zoning Trends**

  Local politics and rezonings tend to ebb and flow based upon current local leadership and the level of community involvement. Be sure to track rezonings around your property to better understand the potential for your land. This is also critical relative to rezoning your property for higher-density uses. Density equals value.

- **Highest and Best Use**

  When you begin thinking about the highest and best use, start by considering who could potentially gain the most value from your property. Refer to Strategy #6 for more details on determining the highest and best use, or feel free to contact us to brainstorm different ideas.

- **Demographic Trends**

  Evaluate demographic trends within your submarket to determine if an area's population is growing, increasing in income, aging, declining in household income, or losing residents.

  Changes in these indicators may signal that it may be a good time to sell as new opportunities for potential uses or product types increase in viability. For example, if the surrounding population is aging, senior housing may become a profitable option for new development.

- **Schools**

  The quality of the schools that serve your area has a massive impact on a property's value, especially if you are zoned for and plan to position your land for either multi-family or single-family housing.

Apartment developers look closely at the quality of elementary schools because apartments tend to house families with younger children. Single-family developers focus more on the quality of high schools. As mentioned in an earlier chapter, a helpful resource to determine the quality of your schools is *greatschools.com*. It ranks all the schools in Georgia and shows how your area's schools compare with others around the state.

- **Comparables**

When you begin thinking about selling your property, one of the first things to look at is pricing for available, under contract, and sold comparable properties. These are often referred to as comps. Comparable sold properties are the most reliable way to determine value.

Comps give you an idea of what the market is willing to pay for similar properties. This will provide you with a good indication of what your property could sell for and where to start in terms of pricing. Pricing is a combination of art and science.

An experienced broker knows that there are many other factors that, as we have discussed in this book, can influence price. Therefore, be sure to ask your broker for a BOV or broker opinion of value. A BOV will allow the broker to present the case for a value that is based on comps but also considers other factors that could increase demand for your specific property, such as rezonings or new developments.

- **Future Developments**

  It is important to be aware of and understand the new developments that are being proposed near your property. As already noted, these developments could include residential, commercial, industrial, schools, parks, or mixed-use projects. By tracking the new projects, you can better anticipate how your property's value could be affected.

  Keep your ears open for conversations about new activity and developments being discussed, officially and unofficially, in planning meetings and the chamber.

  Be supportive of rezonings that can enhance the value of your property, and be vocal in opposing any rezonings that could negatively impact the value or marketability of your land.

- **Developer**

  Sometimes the decision by a developer to acquire land in a particular area is driven by wanting to enter a new market. If that is the case, they may value the opportunity more, and as such, be willing to pay more to get their foot in the door of a growing or particularly opportunistic market. On the other hand, if a competing developer already has multiple deals or holdings in a market, they may not have the same appetite or flexibility as the new-to-market prospective buyer.

MARKET VALUE CHECKLIST

Understanding what impacts the market value of your property is challenging. Here is a checklist to guide you in the process.

- Is the area surrounding your property transitioning in a desirable manner?
- Are there new product types emerging in your submarket that may lead you to think outside the box concerning potential uses?
- Are there new employment centers coming to your area?
- Is your area seeing significant growth?
- Do you know the comps in your submarket?

- Who would gain the most from acquiring your land? Who is your ideal buyer?
- Are there other comparable properties for sale in your area?
- Are there unique attributes to your property that could positively or adversely affect its value?
- Is the current governing body of your area pro-growth or anti-growth?

Considerations

- **Supply and Demand:** The supply of available undeveloped property within your submarket will dramatically impact the value of your land. As demand increases and supply decreases, prices will rise.
- **Location**: A great location can overcome many property imperfections.
- **Track the Trends:** Be aware of the trends affecting your submarket. These trends include new designs and products, demographic changes, and zoning regulations.

Key Takeaways

1. Study the projects within your submarket that may impact your property's value.

2. Communicate your support at city and county meetings for rezonings that can enhance the value of your property.

3. Comps are an essential guide to pricing and potential value, but they only tell you part of the story. Stay informed and work with a creative and reputable broker to maximize the value of your land.

EXPERIENCE FROM THE FIELD

The Gwinnett Wishbone

When I first started my career in Gwinnett County, the area between I-85 and State Route 316 was known as the Gwinnett Wishbone.

All the properties between those routes were very desirable, and we sold multiple tracts of land along those corridors. In 1986, while working with Property Systems Corporation, we sold 432 acres at the intersection of I-85 and State Route 316 for $30,000,000. This was one of the largest land transactions in metro Atlanta in 1986. The property was ultimately developed into a mixed-use project with office warehouse, retail, and apartment complexes.

Site in Gwinnett sold for $30 million
432-acre tract is at the juncture of Interstate 85 and Highway 316

By Sallye Salter
Staff Writer

A prime site near Gwinnett Place Mall has been purchased for $30 million by mortgage banking giant Lomas & Nettleton Financial Group for its first Atlanta development and by a Mississippi firm that last year bought the Darlington Apartments and 4,000 acres in Cherokee County.

The seller of the 432 acres was B.F. Saul Real Estate Investment Trust, a Washington, D.C., firm that for several years has been developing Circle 75, an office-commercial complex in the Cumberland area of Cobb County.

The Gwinnett land, at the juncture of Interstate 85 and Highway 316, has frontage on those roads plus Satellite Boulevard, Highway 120 and Boggs Road.

The Lomas & Nettleton development arm that bought 225 acres of the land is "pursuing" purchase of several other metropolitan Atlanta sites for residential and commercial projects, said Alexander L. Buck, Assistant Vice President.

The Bailey-Goodwin Co., which purchased the remaining 207 acres, is putting it up for sale in smaller parcels.

Richard J. Uberto, President of Property Systems Corp., an Atlanta brokerage firm that handled the transaction and is marketing the Bailey-Goodwin parcels, said most of the B.F. Saul tract is zoned for industrial use, but he expects parts of it to be used for commercial-retail projects, including a hotel, over the next several years.

Lomas & Nettleton, which has named its project Pinebrook Commerce Center, has parcels for sale at prices ranging from $95,000 to $140,000 per acre.

Uberto said the land had been owned by B.F. Saul for about two decades and was among the metropolitan Atlanta sites originally considered as a location for the Atlanta Merchandise Mart, the Atlanta stadium and, more recently, the Gwinnett regional mall.

Bailey-Goodwin, based in Jackson, Miss., made its first move into the Atlanta market last year with the $16 million purchase of the 17-story Darlington Apartments on Peachtree Road. The firm, which later purchased and resold 4,000 acres in Cherokee for a residential complex, also has acquired tracts on Interstate 20 east and west of the city.

432-acre land sale at the intersection of I-85 and State Route 316

EXPERIENCE FROM THE FIELD

Tucker Timeline Turnaround

The city of Tucker was incorporated in 2015. It is in DeKalb County and has great access to I-285 and I-85. There are few tracts of land that are more than 10 acres in the city. We had the privilege of working with a family who wanted to sell their 25 acres.

Due to the lack of supply, there was strong demand, and we generated five offers to purchase the property. This strengthened our position to negotiate beneficial terms for our owner.

Three of the offers were from national home builders who demanded a protracted and conditional timeline based upon their ability to obtain a land disturbance permit (LDP). The process of obtaining the permit is lengthy and can be unpredictable. Accepting those terms would have eliminated my client's ability to manage the transaction's timeline effectively.

With that in mind, we chose to do the deal with a well-capitalized smaller builder/developer who agreed to our timeframe and did not make the contract subject to obtaining a land disturbance permit.

To the benefit of the seller, the property sold in 2021 without a land disturbance permit.

EXPERIENCE FROM THE FIELD

Rowen Development to Spur Innovation & Growth

In 2020, Gwinnett County announced its largest development in the county's history, a 2,000-acre mixed-use project modeled after the Research Triangle in North Carolina.

Known as the Rowen Development, the project will be located between Atlanta, Athens, and Gainesville, with more than two miles of road frontage on each side of State Route 316.

The vision for the project is to transform scientific research in three of the state's biggest economic drivers—agriculture, medicine, and environmentally conscious industries. The research facilities aim to draw talent, people, and ideas from the 50 educational institutions that are within an hour's drive of the area.

The project will also be within driving distance from more than 50 Fortune 1000 headquarters and is expected to create over 18,500 jobs by 2035 and as many as 100,000 jobs long term. Thus, the development will benefit the targeted industries as well as the region's population, economy, and businesses for decades to come.

Well done, Gwinnett County!

Gwinnett planning nearly 2,000-acre research park on SR 316, as many as 100,000 jobs expected to be generated

By Curt Yeomans curt.yeomans@gwinnettdailypost.com   August 25, 2020

Rowen, by the numbers

Size: Nearly 2,000 acres

Jobs created by 2035: 18,500

Jobs created when fully built out: 80,000-100,000

Annual labor income by 2035: $1,655 billion

Annual labor income when fully built out: $8 billion to $10 billion

Construction costs by 2035: $1.15 billion

Construction costs once fully built out: $6.89 billion

Development Bonds to pay for project: $70 million

Gwinnett County officials are planning a major medical, environmental and agricultural mixed-use research park in Dacula and Auburn area that is expected to rival the Research Triangle Park in the Raleigh-Durham area of North Carolina and Tech Square in Atlanta.

The nearly 2,000-acre development, known as Rowen, will be located along more than two miles of State Route 316 on the Gwinnett side of the Gwinnett-Barrow County line. A map of the site shows it will stretch northward to Winder Highway at the county line.

Research parks are places where multiple companies locate and set up scientific and technological facilities to conduct research for new developments and innovations in their respective fields, but Gwinnett officials see a mixed-use community being developed within Rowen as well.

Gwinnett Daily Post article published August 2020

STRATEGY #10
EVALUATE POTENTIAL TAX CONSEQUENCES

Disclaimer: *Tax laws are complex and fluid. At North Georgia Land, Inc., we do not provide tax, legal, or accounting advice. This material has been prepared for informational purposes only and is not intended to provide—or be relied upon—for tax, legal, or accounting advice. You should consult your attorney, tax advisor, accountant, and/or CPA for any tax-related, accounting, or legal matters before engaging in* *any transaction.* **At the printing of this book, the current administration is considering changing many of the tax laws discussed below.**

There are many tax consequences related to owning and selling property. Be sure to calculate the potential tax ramifications with your tax advisor early in the process to help minimize the taxable gain and evaluate other potential opportunities.

In this chapter, we offer a checklist of items to be considered and discussed with your accountant and other relevant advisors regarding your land. Keep in mind that the list is only a starting point and not intended to be all-inclusive in its scope.

- *Should you place your property in a Conservation Use Value Assessment Program?*

  The program, sometimes referred to as CUVA, allows landowners to potentially reduce their property taxes. According to the Georgia Department of Revenue's Conservation Use Assessment page, the following guidance is offered:

  Owners of agricultural land, timberland, and environmentally sensitive land may qualify for conservation use assessment under O.C.G.A.

Section 48-5-7.4. The Georgia Revenue Commissioner has the responsibility of annually determining the values for ad valorem tax purposes of this type of land and publishing rules and regulations to help county tax assessors determine the values of property that qualify for conservation use assessment.

Conservation use property is assessed at 40% of current use value, which gives a reduced assessment to the owner of this type of property when compared to other property assessed at 40% of fair market value. This favorable tax treatment is designed to protect these property owners from being pressured by the property tax burden to convert their land from agricultural use to residential or commercial use, hence the name "conservation use" assessment. In return for the favorable tax treatment, the property owner must keep the land undeveloped in a qualifying use for a period of ten years or incur stiff penalties. Owners who breach their conservation use covenant must pay back to the taxing authorities twice the savings they have received over the life of the covenant up to the point it was breached.

Source: Georgia Department of Revenue, Conservation Use Assessment page;

https://dor.georgia.gov/conservation-use-assessment-information

While the CUVA offers guidance, each state has its own requirements. Consult your county tax assessor and tax advisor to better understand your potential tax savings and the requirements of the CUVA Program.

If your property is placed in a CUVA Program and you sell your property before its expiration, you <u>may</u> be responsible for rollback taxes and penalties. Although each case is unique, we have on occasion required that the purchaser of the land pay any resulting rollback taxes and penalties, or we work with the local tax assessor's office to explore other ways of avoiding the penalties.

- ***Did you inherit the property?***

  If you did, it is important to have an appraisal at the time of death. This will establish a new and higher cost basis for the property and help lower your taxes at the time of sale. This appraisal at the time of death should be done regardless of whether you are selling your land or not. Once again, check with your CPA relative to this issue. **Tax laws may have changed since the publishing of this book.**

- *Is the subject property your primary residence?*

  If it is, and you are married and filing jointly, the IRS may offer a tax benefit. The amount of that exemption could be higher depending on the cost basis of your property. These benefits change over time and may be impacted by your situation. Consult your tax advisor before making any decisions.

- *Is a 1031 Exchange right for you?*

  Typically, costs such as maintenance, taxes, and security are associated with owning property, even if it is raw land. To convert a non-income producing asset into an income-producing asset, we have many clients who choose to sell their land and acquire property that will generate an income stream.

  To further maximize their advantage, many of our clients leverage IRS Code Section 1031, popularly known as a 1031 Exchange, to indefinitely defer any capital gains taxes upon the sale of their property. There is no limit to the number of exchanges an investor can make. However, the 1031 rule does have strict time-lines and other parameters that must be followed. **Consult your tax advisor for more information. Tax laws may have changed since the publishing of this book.**

Many of our clients sell their raw land and use the proceeds via a 1031 Exchange to purchase a triple net lease property that provides them with a relatively passive income stream. Triple net lease properties are those in which the lease stipulates that the tenant, not the owner, is responsible for paying the property's expenses, including taxes, insurance, and maintenance. Many of these sites are well-located and have national or regional credit tenants.

For example, you could acquire a land parcel with a quick-service restaurant as a tenant on a triple net lease. The tenant would be responsible for all improvements, expenses, taxes, insurance, and maintenance—not you. Your only job is to receive your monthly stream of income in the form of a rent check. A triple net lease property is a great passive income stream option for many owners to consider.

Key Takeaways

1. Meet with your CPA and other relevant tax, legal, and accounting advisors before making any decisions. Laws can change quickly.

2. If you inherited the property, meet with your attorney and tax advisor to make sure you get a *date of death appraisal*. Check the current laws prior to getting an appraisal.

3. If selling, consider a 1031 Exchange. You can use your exchange to invest in additional raw land in the path of growth or in a triple net lease.

4. Look into the CUVA option to minimize property taxes.

STRATEGY #11

IDENTIFY AND MITIGATE POTENTIAL LEGAL ISSUES AND RISKS

Disclaimer*: Our team at North Georgia Land, Inc. works daily with landowners, but we are not lawyers or insurance specialists and recommend you consult your lawyer and insurance advisors concerning your unique situation. Below is a checklist of considerations specific to landowners.*

Land ownership is a big responsibility. There are numerous legal issues and risks associated with buying, owning, and selling property. In this chapter, we will look at some of the ways you can protect yourself, your neighbors, and your property from some of these risks.

- **General Liability Insurance**

  As the landowner, you are responsible for anything that happens on your property, including
  someone getting hurt. It does not matter if you
  are actively using your land or not. If someone
  is injured while on your land, a general liability
  insurance policy will help provide you with financial protection. If you allow people to hunt
  or use recreational vehicles on your property,
  there is additional risk associated with this use.

  Be sure to consult your insurance agent and
  other relevant advisors to confirm that you have
  adequate coverage to protect you in the event of
  an accident. In addition, keep your property
  gated to limit access from potential trespassers.

- **Attractive Nuisance**

  An "attractive nuisance" is something on your
  property that is likely to attract children or teens
  that could potentially cause them harm or be
  dangerous. If injury or harm does occur to a
  child or teen on your property, you could be
  held liable. Items and scenarios could include
  but are not limited to abandoned cars, piles of
  lumber, trampolines, large appliances, empty or
  filled swimming pools, etc.

These and other risks make it crucial to discuss liability insurance and the possible need for an umbrella policy with your insurance agent. An umbrella policy provides you with additional protection beyond the coverage of your under-lying policies. It is relatively inexpensive and offers additional peace of mind.

Be sure to consult your insurance agent and other relevant advisors regarding your property and to confirm that you have adequate coverage to protect you in the event of an accident.

Junked vehicles can attract children or teens.
Photo Credit: Unsplash

Old appliances, TVs, and tires are examples
of potential attractive nuisances.
Photo Credit: Unsplash

- **Hazardous Materials**

  As mentioned in the previous chapters, it is essential to walk your property regularly. This is a great opportunity to make sure no one is trespassing and dumping potentially hazardous materials on your land.

  Environmental issues have become a very litigious topic and patrolling your land and limiting access will help ensure it stays free of trespassers. We have found that even posting "No Trespassing" signs along visible entry points is a good deterrent to keep people off your land.

Post "No Trespassing" signs at multiple
locations around your property.
Photo Credit: Unsplash

- **Dead or Dying Trees**

  It is a good idea to remove dead or dying trees,
  particularly along your property lines. If a tree
  on your land falls onto your neighbor's property, it could damage a fence, a car, or other improvements, and you could be held liable. Make
  sure you get insurance and remove any visibly
  dying trees that are along property lines.

- **Easements**

  If you have granted utility easements, access
  easements, or road improvement easements,
  keep all your files together and secure and make
  copies that you keep in a separate location. This

will help if you decide to sell all or a portion of your property.

EXPERIENCE FROM THE FIELD
Multiple 55-Gallon Drums on Property

We sold a property in North Georgia that had several 55-gallon drums located on the land.

The drums were empty and being stored on site. When we signed the listing agreement, I requested that the owners remove the drums. Unfortunately, the owners did not remove the drums.

Once the property was under contract, the purchaser's environmental engineer completed a Phase 1 environmental report. However, because the 55-gallon drums were on the property, a Phase 2 environmental report, which involves testing soils in and around the drums, was also required. The Phase 2 report created an additional cost to the developer and slowed down the closing.

Had the empty 55-gallon drums been removed, the Phase 2 testing would not have been required, the buyer would have been spared the expense, and the transaction would have closed more quickly.

Typical 55-gallon drums
Photo Credit: Unsplash

Key Takeaways

1. Meet with your insurance agent to understand your liability exposure and update your insurance.
2. Post "No Trespassing" signs at key entry points to your property.
3. Remove dead trees and other hazards from your property that may cause harm or be considered a liability.

STRATEGY #12
NEGOTIATING NUGGETS

L and transactions are complicated, and millions of dollars are often at stake. Therefore, these contracts require a high level of experience and legal counsel. To avoid conflict and the threat of legal action, it is crucial to be well represented by a competent and experienced commercial land broker.

Although we always go into a negotiation hoping all parties will be reasonable and the contract will be clear, if this is your first rodeo, the process can be confusing. Below are a few critical items that should be considered when negotiating a contract. This is not an exhaustive list, and negotiations should be handled with extreme care.

When negotiating a contract, be aware of the following:

1. Ensure that the buyer is financially qualified to make the acquisition, has a proven track record, and a solid reputation. Conduct proper due diligence on your buyer.
2. Request the developer run title and survey the property during the due diligence period.
3. Limit the due diligence period to a reasonable period. That period depends on the anticipated use of the property and the complexity of the transaction.
4. Always use calendar days as opposed to business days to minimize confusion.
5. When your contract is subject to rezoning, determine your rezoning application deadline. We suggest requiring the buyer submit his/her rezoning application two days before the local county or city's rezoning deadline. This gives the purchaser an opportunity to correct any errors in the application without missing the deadline.
6. Stagger the earnest money deposits throughout the contract as conditions are satisfied.
7. Have an escrow agent (either a title company or an attorney) hold the earnest money deposit(s).

8. Make sure you are selling your property with a limited warranty deed instead of a general warranty deed. Limited warranty deeds provide more protection to the owner.

9. Request the purchaser to be responsible for any rollback taxes. For example, CUVA breaches may trigger rollback taxes. See Strategy #10 for more details.

10. Be conscious of contracts being subject to development permitting approval. This is a common request but often creates delays that are hard to control and conditioned upon the municipality's responsiveness. It can also be delayed by the buyer's engineer or other unforeseen complications. It is better to have clear and tight timeframes to minimize ambiguity that can cause problems and derail the sale.

11. Be aware of contracts being assignable prior to closing.

12. Request that all due diligence materials be released to you in the event the contract is terminated.

13. Establish an outside closing date that will keep the contract from being extended indefinitely.

14. If the property is owned by multiple owners, consider having a legally binding operating agreement that will simplify obtaining the required signatures throughout the process.

15. At closing, most attorneys will require original signatures from all the owners to execute the deeds and closing documents.

16. If you are selling your primary residence, create a post-occupancy agreement to allow you adequate time to remove all your personal belongings from the property after closing. This point is often forgotten but is critical.

17. Verbal agreements are not binding. Everything must be in writing.

18. There will be bumps in the road and unforeseen challenges, that is why it's critical to be well represented and choose your buyer carefully.

EXPERIENCE FROM THE FIELD

Clear & Tight Timeframes Matter

I recently became aware of a transaction that required the purchaser to obtain a land disturbance permit (LDP) as a condition of closing.

Unfortunately, the owner did not establish a timeframe for the purchaser to submit, pursue, and obtain the LDP. There was no outside closing date established in the contract. This allowed the purchaser to extend the agreement indefinitely, and it became a legal point of contention. This could have been avoided if the seller included a tight timeframe and an outside closing date in the agreement.

I was not a participant in this transaction.

Key Takeaways

1. Make sure the buyer is financially qualified, has a proven track record, and a solid reputation.
2. Have a clear and tight timeframe to minimize ambiguity in the process, including an outside closing date.
3. Verbal agreements are not binding. Make sure you get everything in writing.

STRATEGY #13

SELECT THE RIGHT BROKER

The commercial land brokerage business is demanding and complex. Selecting the right broker to help you buy or sell your land may be the most critical decision you will make in the process. There are, however, key characteristics that distinguish the best brokers.

Some of you may be about to embark on the single most important transaction in your family's life, while others may have inherited a portfolio of properties and are not sure where to turn.

Since 1984, I have worked with some of the best brokers in the industry and understand what distinguishes one broker from the next. Not all brokers are equal.

As the steward of your land and the protector of your family's legacy, the decision to hire the right broker is of paramount importance. As you interview brokers, measure them against these nine key qualities.

1. An Authentic Desire to Help You Succeed

A good broker will strive to understand the goals and objectives of all the stakeholders involved in the land transaction. Stakeholders include family members, partners, and other advisors. A good broker will never lose sight of who is the ultimate decision maker—YOU! Good brokers present ideas, solutions, and strategies, but they must always defer to the property owner for the final decision. In a good broker-landowner relationship, the desires and motivations of both parties remain aligned. Your protection and satisfaction should be the broker's ultimate desire.

2. Integrity and Trustworthiness

This seems like an obvious characteristic, but in real life, it is not as easy to distinguish. The best way to evaluate a broker is to look at the broker's track record and past dealings. Ask for referrals, speak with the referrers directly, inquire around town, and trust your gut.

3. Local Knowledge

Each county and municipality throughout our great state is unique. A broker with local knowledge can provide insight into the probability of having the property rezoned, who the best attorneys are in the area, and the best buyers for your property.

4. Years of Experience

There is no education like the school of hard knocks. Brokers must be patient, intuitive, and know when and how to ask the right questions. These skills can only be developed from first-hand experiences solving a vast array of challenges in complex land transactions.

5. Specialization

If you are selling land, work with an experienced and reputable land broker. Do not offer the listing to your brother-in-law because he has a real estate license or give it to a broker that does not specialize exclusively in the sale of land. The difference in their knowledge will translate to a difference in the dollars you put in your pocket.

6. Network of Contacts

Every real estate transaction encounters challenges. Having the right contacts, including active buyers, builders, attorneys, consultants, county personnel, contractors, accountants, title companies, etc., will help smooth out rough spots along the way.

7. A Solid Reputation

Reputation is everything. Check the broker's reputation, referrals, and a history of their past transactions. It may seem a bit tedious, but once you do your research, you will have the opportunity to build a long-term business relationship with someone you trust. You may be surprised at how easy it is to learn information about brokers in the land business.

8. Vision and Creativity

As many of the examples I shared with you demonstrate, most transactions require various degrees of patience, vision, and creativity. Many of the challenges faced in obtaining the highest possible value for your land require a great deal of problem solving. Whether it is re-zoning, annexations, obtaining utilities for the property, or the impact of new road improvements, these issues demand creativity, vision, and expertise.

9. Patience

A seasoned broker understands that land transactions are complex. Therefore, it is critical to be patient and persevering to navigate the political and economic winds that impact each decision. Patience allows for a time-out and a chance to regroup and explore alternatives. Pushing politicians or county officials too hard rarely delivers the desired outcome.

It is important for me to mention that if the broker you are interviewing does not have these qualities and others you have outlined for yourself, you are not being rude by not hiring them. Even if they are someone you are related to, was referred to you by a friend, or is someone you've done business with in the past, you owe it to yourself and your family to hire the most competent professional for your situation. Choosing the right broker means you are being a responsible steward of your land and protecting your family's legacy.

About Off-Market Deals

Many owners are tempted to sell their property off-market directly to a buyer because they believe they can save the commission. While that may be true, creating buyer competition is one of the broker's most important activities and will ultimately get you the highest price. In the end, the higher price will likely make up for the difference in the commission. Remember the point discussed in Strategy #9:

> *Sometimes the decision by a developer to acquire land in a particular area is driven by wanting to enter a new market. If that is the case, they may value the opportunity more, and as such, be willing to pay more to get their foot in the door of a growing or particularly opportunistic area. However, if a competing developer already has multiple deals or holdings in a market, they may not have the same appetite or flexibility as the new-to-market prospective buyer, and rarely would an owner know this information.*

Although price is a primary consideration, many other factors are critical to the overall success of a transaction. Some of these include the likelihood of rezoning, the complexity of obtaining permits, and the time frames associated with each stage of the process.

In addition, a good broker will protect your interests and make sure you are not entering into an agreement or situation that puts you at risk. A reputable and experienced broker that specializes in selling land can help you properly navigate the process.

EXPERIENCE FROM THE FIELD

It's About the Small Things

In the spring of 2014, I met a woman named Doris, who owned a 45-acre tract of land in Forsyth County.

She grew up during the Great Depression and was widowed with no children or close family members. She hired me to represent her in the sale of her property. Our friendship grew as we overcame multiple challenges related to rezoning, annexation, and obtaining utility easements. We ultimately sold her property.

Throughout the process, her health started to decline. Her illness had not been properly diagnosed, and I began taking her to her doctor appointments. After multiple visits, we ended up in the office of a gastroenterologist who determined that Doris had stomach cancer. During this time, she shared with me that her will and estate were not in proper order. I helped her identify a good attorney that could update her will.

My wife and I would visit her regularly to care for her during her last few years of life. She passed away in February of 2017. Doris was more than a landowner; she became a close friend.

"My family owned 45 acres in Forsyth County for over 100 years. Unfortunately, most of my relatives had died, and I needed someone to guide me through the local politics to help me obtain the highest possible price. Bruce had the needed relationships to get the property rezoned, obtain the necessary utility easements, minimize my taxes, and close the transaction. Bruce and his team went the extra mile to help me plan my estate. Thanks, Bruce."
—Doris

CHOOSING A BROKER CHECKLIST

In addition to the nine qualities we listed previously, below is a checklist with questions to ask when interviewing a broker.

1. Do they specialize *only* in land?
2. How many years have they been in the business?
3. What professional designations do they hold?
4. Do you sense he or she is enthusiastic about your property?

5. Does the broker have strong local knowledge of the market and local politics?

6. Do they understand the unique characteristics of your land?

7. Does the broker understand your goals and concerns?

8. Have they demonstrated vision, creativity, patience, and perseverance in past deals? Ask them to share case studies with you.

9. Does the broker have existing buyer contacts so they can deal directly with the buyers and potentially reduce the amount of commission you pay?

10. Does the broker have trusted relationships with other team members that may be required to close your transaction such as certified public accountants, land planners, civil engineers, environmental engineers, zoning attorneys, etc.? This can save you a great deal of time and expense. Be sure, however, to independently vet all recommendations.

11. Can the broker help you and your family create the legacy you desire?

CONCLUSION

Since 1984, I've had the privilege of working with landowners throughout Atlanta and its suburbs. I've seen the good, the bad, and the ugly and have lived through many real estate cycles. Atlanta and the people who live here continue to be resilient, forward-thinking, and creative in developing real estate.

One of my favorite parts of the process is hearing the stories of parents, grandparents, and great-grandparents who have had dreams about their property and have passed them down through the generations. In addition, I have witnessed the unique ways that landowners and developers have honored those who have gone before us.

For instance, in 2001, land developer and World War II veteran D. Scott Hudgens Jr. donated 775 acres in

Cherokee County to establish Georgia National Cemetery. The cemetery honors our United States Military Veterans and their families.

Even closer to home, D. Scott Hudges, Jr. donated land and resources to Peachtree Christian Hospice in Duluth. This hospice facility is where my dad spent his last days. It provided a level of care and dignity that made his final days peaceful and grace-filled.

Many owners have left their mark on the community through naming opportunities or establishing local parks and gardens that will stand the test of time. Others have used the proceeds of their land sales to support their children or grandchildren's education, help a newlywed couple with a down payment, or donate to their favorite charity.

Others choose to use the proceeds to create memorable vacation experiences for their families. These could include a white-water rafting trip down the Snake River, a dude Ranch out west, a trip to Hawaii that you've dreamed about for years, or a cruise through the Greek Islands or the Norwegian Fjords.

Owning land is an opportunity and a privilege. It provides us with the potential to create wealth and build family memories. As property owners, we are stewards of a precious and unique resource, our land. No two properties are identical, and every tract should be cared for and appreciated. Land can impact multiple generations.

Keep this book handy as a reference guide and resource to help you better manage your property and maximize its value. If we can be of service to you or your family, please give us a call at 678-770-4146.

We wish you and your family only the best!

ABOUT THE AUTHOR

Bruce M. Carlisle, CCIM

A native Atlantan, Bruce Carlisle began his commercial real estate career in 1984. In 1993, after many years of working at some of the top land brokerage and development firms in Georgia, including Property Systems Corporation, The Trammell Crow Company, and The Scott Hudgens Company, he launched North Georgia Land, Inc.

His mission with North Georgia Land is to help landowners and developers reach their goals and maximize their wealth through land management, sales, and acquisitions.

Throughout his career, Mr. Carlisle has been guided by the belief that just as every parcel of land has unique qualities and characteristics, every property owner and family has a unique set of goals, dreams, and desires. This principle has led Mr. Carlisle to seek to understand the individual goals of landowners and their vision for their property, portfolio, and family.

More importantly, this understanding has allowed him to develop long-lasting relationships with landowners, consultants, and other property stakeholders that have transcended generations.

Mr. Carlisle's commitment to delivering practical experience and the highest level of expertise in commercial real estate drove him to seek the CCIM designation (Certified Commercial Investment Member). CCIMs are recognized as experts in the commercial real estate field. This designation is earned by completing a graduate-level curriculum, including technology courses, advanced training in negotiating real estate deals, and other specialized commercial real estate courses. In addition, each CCIM candidate must present a portfolio of qualifying transactions and work product demonstrating a proven level of high-performance, as well as pass a rigorous exam testing the candidate's mastery of the concepts introduced through the CCIM courses. Mr. Carlisle has held the CCIM designation for more than 25 years.

During his decades in the business, Mr. Carlisle has seen technology dramatically change the commercial brokerage landscape, but it has not changed his core competency of knowing and helping people. As much as his practice employs the latest technology, data, and tools to offer his clients every advantage possible, Mr. Carlisle still relishes the intangible value of personally guiding each of his clients through successful property sales transactions.

Whether he is working with big multinational corporate clients, regional businesses, or local families, Mr. Carlisle appreciates the opportunity he has to touch the lives of countless landowners and help shape the north Georgia landscape.

His corporate clients include some of the country's best-known consumer brands such as Walgreens, Publix, Starbucks, Kroger, and McDonald's, among many others. He has also worked with national and regional builders, including D.R. Horton, Beazer Homes, Lennar, Pulte Homes, Meritage Homes, Taylor Morrison, The Providence Group, Retail Planning Corporation, and many more.

Throughout his career, Mr. Carlisle has successfully closed more than $200 million in land transactions throughout the Atlanta metropolitan area.

While Mr. Carlisle's career is marked by many accomplishments, he considers his greatest achievement to be the legacy he is creating through his marriage and family. In 1984, he married his high school sweetheart, Marybel. They have two wonderful adult children— Zachary and Marina.

Bruce and Marybel reside in Forsyth County, where they are active in their local church and present marriage enrichment retreats several times throughout the year. When he is not in the office, you can find Bruce fishing, gardening, hiking the north Georgia mountains with his wife and their golden retriever, Roxby, or possibly planning his next family adventure abroad.

When his children were young and they asked their dad what he did, his reply was simple, "I sell dirt." Under every great development and every unique project, there lies the same thing–dirt. Bruce is one of the best dirt salesmen in Atlanta.

Zachary and Marina Carlisle and friends playing
on a property Bruce successfully sold

Carlisle family photo from Marina Carlisle and
Drew Mirolli's wedding day

ABOUT NORTH GEORGIA LAND

A t North Georgia Land, we know that you want to be a wise steward of one of your largest assets, your land. To do that, you need a trusted adviser. Many landowners we meet have specialists to help them with their medical, legal, and accounting needs, such as a doctor, lawyer, wealth manager, and CPA. However, they do not have someone to help them with their land. The challenge with commercial real estate is that selling a property can be complicated, and the potential for making a mistake is quite high for the inexperienced. You and your family deserve a proven ally to protect your interests.

At North Georgia Land, we focus exclusively on selling land in the north Georgia area. Our services are specifically tailored to meet the needs of buyers and sellers of undeveloped land throughout Atlanta and its suburbs. These services include:

- Acquisition and disposition of land parcels
- Site selection and evaluation
- Broker Opinion of Value (BOV) and pricing strategies
- Annexations
- Rezonings
- Land development consultations
- Highest and best use determination

Our expertise and experience allow us to understand the complexity of managing land transactions of all sizes. As a family-owned and operated business, we also understand the importance of protecting your family's interests and legacy.

Contact us for a consultation. We are happy to conduct a free assessment, walk you through the process and answer any questions you may have about your specific situation. We can be reached at 678-770-4146.